CCSS Genre Historica

MW00682946

Essential Question
Why is it important to keep a record of the past?

Song and Dance

BY PAUL MASON
ILLUSTRATED BY JORGE SANTILLAN

Chapter 1
A NEW HOME

The family made their way along the crowded Boston city street, their backs bent over with the weight of their belongings.

Patrick Cavanaugh struggled to keep up with his parents because he kept stopping to stare at the buildings. He'd never seen anything like them before. In their village in Ireland, the tallest building was the clock tower, but these huge buildings were at least twice as tall. Patrick felt tiny.

"Patrick, will you keep up, please!" his father, Donal, called from farther up the street. Showing obedience to his father, Patrick hurried to catch up.

Patrick's mother, Mary, smiled at him. "Come on, Patrick, we'll soon see our new home."

"Okay," Patrick replied as he walked a little faster. After having to endure being trapped below deck on a rolling ship for what seemed like years, he liked the idea of finally reaching their destination.

His hopes of finding refuge in a comfortable home soon faded when the landlord showed them into their apartment. "Is this it?" Patrick whispered to his mother as he dropped his heavy bag on the floor.

Patrick's mother looked around the tiny space with its bare walls and old furniture. It wasn't quite what she was expecting, either, but she smiled. "You saw some of the places on the walk here, didn't you? We've got a better place than most people."

Patrick nodded. His mother was right. Away from the grand streets of downtown Boston, it seemed as if the people in this Irish neighborhood were packed together like the crates on the docks. Every building was crammed with people. Even in their apartment, they couldn't escape the sounds of shouting in the street and the dull clattering from the apartment above.

"Now, first things first," said Patrick's father after he'd inspected the apartment with his family. "How about a little music to welcome us to our new home?"

Patrick grinned. He knew his father was going to say that. Patrick asked for his favorite song, "I'll Tell Me Ma."

"A grand idea," laughed his father, "and you can sing." Patrick's dad started them off, the birdlike sound of his whistle dancing around the apartment. Then his mother joined in, her bow bouncing and weaving its way over the violin strings.

Then Patrick began to sing. His father was right. Things did seem better with a little music, although Patrick couldn't escape the fact that their small village and the warm smiles of everyone they knew were a whole ocean away.

Chapter 2

PRECIOUS MUSIC

The following morning, Patrick's parents planned their day. His father's eldest brother, Sean, had told them about a new kind of theater called vaudeville. Uncle Sean had been to a vaudeville theater when he visited America.

Vaudeville was a variety show with musicians, jugglers, and actors. Sean said that some of the theaters even had performances that lasted all day. He figured that theater owners were always looking for new performers.

Patrick really hoped Uncle Sean was right, because his parents had given up everything to make a new start in the United States. They were really counting on getting a job on the vaudeville circuit.

"We'll ask around town," said his father. "We'll introduce ourselves to the theater managers and charm them with a song."

Patrick's mother looked nervous. "Do you think they'll like us?"

"Of course," Patrick's father said, smiling. "They'll be crying out for some traditional ballads."

The first theater they found had a sign on the stage door that said: NO NEW ACTS NEEDED.

"Let's try another one," Patrick's dad said. "Their loss." Even though they shrugged it off, Patrick saw his parents exchange glances.

As they wandered from theater to theater, their concerns grew. Most of the theaters weren't looking for musicians, and some just plain ignored them. Those who were looking for entertainers shook their heads as soon as they found out that the family played traditional Irish music.

"Tin whistles, fiddles, and Irish ballads? Everyone can play those in this town," one of the stage managers told them. When he saw how downcast Patrick's father looked, he added, "You can try O'Hare's, but I bet he'll tell you the same."

They finally found O'Hare's Theater tucked down a side alley. It might have been small, but its lights were blazing, and the sign looked cheerful. Patrick's dad once again presented himself at the backstage door. Although Mr. O'Hare listened patiently, he was about to close the door on them when he noticed Patrick looking tired and upset in the alley.

O'Hare let out a long sigh. "I'll probably find myself bankrupt at this rate, but I'll tell you what. I'll give you a chance in tomorrow's performance. Show me what you can do in front of an audience."

"You won't regret it," said Patrick's dad, shaking hands with him.

That night Patrick's mom laid out their sheet music on the kitchen table. Though his parents knew many songs by heart, these songs were special. They would never be discarded. Some were from Granddad Joseph's collection; they were a gift from him. Some were treasured family favorites, while others had been bought with hard-earned savings. They needed to choose their best music if they were going to impress the audience tomorrow.

"How about 'Last Rose of Summer,'" Patrick suggested. He thought about the last time the whole family, cousins and all, had squeezed into his grandparents' house for a feast. At the end, when their bellies were full and the fire had died down, his parents had started to play that sad melody. He loved hearing his mother's voice singing that beautiful song.

"It's a lovely song," Patrick's father agreed. "What about 'Waxies' Dargle'?" he said, picking up a song sheet. "That song is such fun. Remember where we first sang that one?" he asked, smiling at his wife.

"How could I forget," she replied. "At that theater in New Ross. I can still see the lights of the houses along the harbor. It was such a lovely night."

As they went through the music sheets, each song brought a different piece of home to life. Every song reminded them of another place, another memory. It was as if the music painted a picture. Though they knew how far away they were from Ireland, the past seemed closer with these songs on their lips.

Chapter 3
O'HARE'S THEATER

The following day, the Cavanaugh family arrived at the theater with plenty of time to spare before the start of the performance.

"This is it, Mary," said Patrick's father as he swung open the door.

Backstage, the other performers were already preparing for the show. Some were putting on costumes and make-up in one of the tiny dressing rooms. Others were practicing their lines on stage. A couple of acrobats in bright leotards were doing stretching exercises.

O'Hare's Theater might not have been the grandest theater in the city, but Patrick hadn't been in a place like this before. He admired the red velvet curtains, the gold decorations on the walls, and the comfortable seats in the boxes for those who could afford them. To Patrick, it was all marvelous.

Mr. O'Hare came out from one of the wings. "I see you're here," he smiled. "This afternoon you'll go on after the Costelli brothers, just before the intermission. The stage manager will give you a nod, I'll give an introduction, then it's all up to you."

"Sounds grand," said Patrick's father.

"Come, let me introduce you to some of the other performers," said Mr. O'Hare.

Not long after, Mr. O'Hare opened the box office to sell tickets. A slow stream of people began to take their seats. Patrick's parents waited in the wings for their cue. Patrick could see his father's hands clenching and unclenching, his mother's foot tapping—their nerves were getting the better of them. They may have been musicians all their lives, but so much depended on this afternoon. Patrick tried to cheer them up with a smile, but they both seemed so distant, so worried.

At last the Costelli brothers took the stage. Patrick could hear the audience roaring with laughter as the comedians performed, tumbling around and chasing each other in a mock fight. The audience applauded loudly when they finished.

"That's a tough act to follow," said Patrick's dad, raising his eyebrows.

The Costelli brothers ran off stage, one of them with the remains of a custard pie smeared all over his face. "The audience is all yours," he said, grinning. "All the best!" He shook Patrick's dad's hand.

"Thanks," said his father.

Then Patrick heard Mr. O'Hare introducing them. "Ladies and gentlemen, every now and then an act comes along that depicts the best that Ireland has to offer! I present to you Donal and Mary Cavanaugh from County Wexford!"

Patrick gave them each a quick hug, and the stage manager waved them on. Patrick found a stack of boxes in the wings that he could climb on to get a better view.

"You'll need to be careful not to fall," whispered the stage manager.

"Sitting up here is one thing," thought Patrick, "but the really treacherous place is out on stage—especially if you have stage fright." His stomach churned as he watched his parents struggling to perform, the weight of their nerves crushing them. His father's voice, normally so strong and so proud, was off-key. His mother's fiddle found the wrong notes again and again. They were sinking.

Soon they started losing the audience, and some people in the front row began talking to each other loudly. Patrick detested such rudeness. How could they be so unkind?

Chapter 4
HERE TO STAY

Across the stage, Patrick saw Mr. O'Hare watching from the wings, disappointment written all over his face. The theater owner glanced out at the restless audience and shook his head. He would have to close the curtains on them.

Just then Patrick slipped. He had been leaning forward to get a better view when he lost his balance and fell from the tower of boxes. Patrick landed smartly on his feet, but the momentum had carried him forward. Patrick sprang onto the stage, making a dramatic entrance like an acrobat. His parents turned around for a moment but bravely carried on playing.

Patrick wasn't sure what to do. Should he quickly run offstage and watch his parents continue to struggle, or should he stay and try to help?

Patrick decided to stay. As his father sang, he began to dance around the stage, miming the words coming out of his father's mouth.

Now the audience sat up, they stopped talking, and some of them even began to smile. A child performer— they liked this. As Patrick's parents reached the end of the song, polite applause broke out across the theater.

Hearing the audience's applause, the first since they had come on stage, Patrick's mother quickly whispered to her husband. "Change of plan," she said, nodding toward the audience. "Let Patrick sing and we'll accompany him."

Patrick's dad nodded, pulling out the tin whistle. They needed to keep the audience on their side. "What shall we give them?"

"How about 'Shores of Amerikay,'" Patrick's mother replied hurriedly. She turned to her son. "Can you sing it?" He could do it. He'd heard them play the song a hundred times. Patrick realized that the audience was getting impatient again. With a wink to Patrick's dad, his mom started fiddling and then his father joined in on the whistle.

Patrick cleared his throat, and he began to sing.

I'm bidding farewell to the land of my youth
and the home I love so well.
And the mountains so grand round
my own native land,
I'm bidding them all farewell …

Patrick's heart thumped in his chest. His voice strained to reach beyond the first few rows of the audience. Then, as he sang those words to the sound of his father's whistle and the violin of his mother, Patrick began to stand up tall.

The song was one they'd been given by Granddad Joseph to take with them. It was about an Irishman leaving his country to begin a new life in America. It could have been written about them. Patrick's voice soared to the back of the theater. His parents had a light in their eyes; they could tell that the audience was spellbound.

When Patrick finished and the last note faded away, a cheer broke out in the theater. There were cries of "Bravo!" and row after row of clapping hands. Patrick beamed and took hold of his parent's hands, and they bowed together. Their faces flushed red at the sight of the happy audience. Patrick turned to see Mr. O'Hare clapping, too—and the other performers who had gathered in the wings. They were all happy to see the family succeed.

"'I'll Tell Me Ma'?" Patrick asked his parents over the noise of the applause. "I think they want another."

His parents grinned at each other and began to play. The look on Mr. O'Hare's face told them the Cavanaugh family would be coming back—but with Patrick taking center stage.

Respond to Reading

Summarize

Use important details from *Song and Dance* to summarize the story. Your graphic organizer may help you.

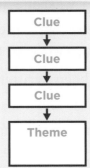

Text Evidence

1. How can you tell that this story is historical fiction?
   GENRE

2. How did Granddad Joseph's songs make the family feel connected to their past? THEME

3. Use context clues to define the word *weight* on page 2. What is a homophone for *weight*? What does the homophone mean? HOMOPHONES

4. Write about Patrick's performance of "Shores of Amerikay." How do details about the song and its effect support the story's theme?
   WRITE ABOUT READING

Compare Texts

Read about Irish immigration to the United States.

In Search of a Better Life

In 1845, a famine began in Ireland. It was caused when a disease destroyed the potato crop. Potatoes were the main source of food for most Irish people, and with no potatoes, many people faced starvation. Tragically, the Great Famine killed nearly one million people in Ireland.

As a result of the famine, many people were forced to leave their homeland. Almost two million Irish people emigrated to the United States between 1845 and 1855 in search of a better life.

Most of the Irish people who moved to the United States were poor and not qualified to do work that paid well. Some were able to find work on the docks, on construction sites, or building railroads. Life was difficult, and living conditions were often unhealthy.

17

While they were trying to build a new life for themselves, the Irish immigrants often turned to their history and culture to give them a sense of belonging in their new community. Irish culture could be found in books and magazines, and on the stage in acts such as vaudeville. Traditional songs were a way to remember home and stay connected to their culture.

Vaudeville Theater

Vaudeville theaters started appearing in the United States in the late 1800s. They quickly became a popular form of live entertainment. A vaudeville show had different artists performing, such as singers, musicians, magicians, and comedians.

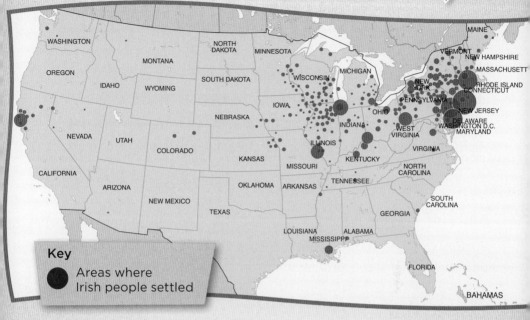

Irish Settlement in the United States as of 1890

Key

Areas where
Irish people settled

Irish immigrants continued to arrive during the late 1880s and early 1900s. Gradually the children and grandchildren of Irish immigrants began to work in more skilled jobs, such as plumbing and boiler making. They also took community jobs, becoming police officers and fire fighters. Some became politicians. Irish immigrants and their descendants have made many important contributions to the United States.

Make Connections

What helped the early immigrants from Ireland feel a sense of community in their new country?
ESSENTIAL QUESTION

Using the map on page 19, find some other places in the United States where Patrick's family could have performed for other Irish immigrants. TEXT TO TEXT

Focus on Literary Elements

Mood Writers use words to help create a mood or atmosphere in a story. This helps readers to visualize and understand the characters' actions and feelings. Writers use words to create a mood that is cheerful, sad, anxious, scary, or dreamy.

Read and Find Reread the description of Patrick's parents on page 10. The writer used words such as *clenching and unclenching*, *distant*, and *worried* to create a dark mood of anxiety.

Reread the description of the family and how they act on page 15. The writer has used words such as *soared*, *light in their eyes*, *beamed*, and *happy* to create a happy and triumphant mood.

Your Turn

Think of four or more different moods a writer might want to show in a story. For each mood, make a word map. Write the name of a mood in the middle of a circle. Draw lines out from the circle and add words that you connect with that mood. For example, if the mood word is *happy*, you could add words such as *giggle*, *laugh*, *grin*, *tickle*, *glad*, or *sunshine*. Share your word maps and save them to help you create atmosphere in your writing.